The Berlin wall

The fall of the Berlin wall

CAITLYN SCOTT

Copyright © 2024 by Caitlyn Scott

Table of contents

Introduction

Welcome to a journey through one of the most dramatic and consequential moments of the 20th century - the fall of the Berlin Wall. Prepare to be captivated, exhilarated, and moved as we delve into the intricacies of this monumental event that reshaped the course of history.

Imagine a world divided, not just by borders, but by ideologies so stark they seemed insurmountable. East versus West, communism versus capitalism, a simmering Cold War threatening to boil over at any moment. Against this backdrop of tension and distrust stood a concrete barrier, a physical manifestation of the ideological divide slicing through the heart of Berlin.

But within the cracks of this imposing structure lay the seeds of change, quietly germinating until they burst forth with irresistible force. Our journey begins long before the first brick was laid, tracing the complex history of post-World War II Germany, the rise of the Iron Curtain, and the simmering discontent simmering beneath the surface.

As we traverse the pages of this narrative, you'll witness the courage of ordinary citizens who dared to dream of freedom, the strategic maneuvers of world leaders navigating the treacherous waters of geopolitics, and the sheer jubilation that erupted when the Wall finally crumbled before the will of the people.

But this is more than just a story of political upheaval; it's a testament to the indomitable human spirit and the power of hope to overcome even the most formidable obstacles. It's a reminder that, even in the darkest of times, the promise of a better tomorrow can inspire acts of bravery and defiance that echo through the ages.

So, dear reader, prepare to be transported back in time to a moment when the world held its breath, when the impossible became possible, and when the bonds of division were shattered in a euphoric explosion of unity. Join us on this odyssey through triumph and tribulation, and discover for yourself why the fall of the Berlin Wall remains an enduring symbol of hope, resilience, and the enduring quest for freedom.

In the annals of history, there are moments that define epochs, turning points where the trajectory of humanity pivots on the axis of fate. The fall of the Berlin Wall stands as one such epochal event, a seismic rupture in the fabric of global politics that reverberated far beyond the streets of Berlin.

But what makes this moment so compelling, so irresistibly captivating, is not just the geopolitical significance or the sheer audacity of the act itself. It's the human drama that unfolded against the backdrop of barbed wire and concrete, the stories of courage, sacrifice, and resilience that transformed a physical barrier into a symbol of oppression and, ultimately, liberation.

As we embark on this journey through time, prepare to meet the visionaries and the dreamers who dared to defy the status quo, the activists and dissidents who risked everything for the chance to breathe free air, and the countless unnamed heroes whose acts of defiance chipped away at the foundations of tyranny.

But our story is not confined to the streets of Berlin or the corridors of power; it's a tapestry woven from the threads of countless lives, each one a testament to the enduring power of the human spirit. From the bustling cafes of East Berlin to the corridors of the Kremlin, from the halls of power in Washington to the humble homes of ordinary citizens, the echoes of this momentous event reverberate still, reminding us of the heights we can reach when we stand united in pursuit of a common goal.

So, dear reader, prepare to be transported across time and space to a moment when history hung in the balance and the fate of nations rested on the shoulders of brave men and women who refused to accept the world as it was. Join us as we uncover the untold stories, unravel the hidden truths, and explore the profound legacy of a wall that once divided a city but ultimately united a world.

Chapter One

The Division Of Germany

In the tumultuous aftermath of World War II, Germany emerged as the epicenter of a new kind of conflict - a Cold War waged not with bullets and bombs, but with ideologies and influence. With the defeat of Nazi Germany, the victorious Allied powers - the United States, Soviet Union, Great Britain, and France - faced the daunting task of rebuilding a shattered continent and charting a course for the future.

However, the seeds of discord had already been sown, as the wartime alliance between the Western Allies and the Soviet Union gave way to suspicion and rivalry. Nowhere was this division more pronounced than in Germany, which found itself carved into occupation zones by the victorious powers.

In 1949, this division became official with the establishment of two separate German states: the Federal Republic of Germany (West Germany) and the German Democratic Republic (East Germany). West Germany aligned itself with the Western powers, embracing democracy and capitalism, while East Germany fell under the sway of the Soviet Union, becoming a bastion of communism in the heart of Europe.

The division of Germany was more than just a geopolitical reality; it was a microcosm of the broader East-West conflict that would come to define the latter half of the 20th century. The Iron Curtain descended across the continent, separating not just East from West, but freedom from oppression, democracy from dictatorship.

For the people of Berlin, this division was felt most acutely. The city, located deep within the heart of East Germany, became a flashpoint in the Cold War struggle, its streets patrolled by soldiers, its skyline dominated by watchtowers and barbed wire.

But even as the physical barriers went up, the desire for reunification burned bright in the hearts of many Germans, both East and West. The division of Germany was not seen as permanent, but as a temporary aberration, an obstacle to be overcome on the path to a united and prosperous future.

Little did they know that the key to reunification would lie not in the halls of power, but in the streets of Berlin itself. The fall of the Berlin Wall would mark not just the reunification of a divided city, but the dawn of a new era in German history - an era defined not by division and conflict, but by unity and reconciliation.

The division of Germany after World War II wasn't just a line drawn on a map; it was a wound that cut deep into the heart of the nation, tearing families apart and sundering communities. With the defeat of Nazi Germany in 1945, the once-powerful nation lay in ruins, its cities reduced to rubble and its spirit shattered by the horrors of war.

In the scramble to rebuild Europe, Germany found itself at the center of a power struggle between the United States and the Soviet Union, the two emerging superpowers of the post-war world. The Potsdam Conference in 1945 saw the division of Germany into four occupation zones, each administered by one of the victorious Allied powers. But what began as a temporary measure soon solidified into a permanent division, as ideological differences and geopolitical rivalries deepened the rift between East and West. In 1949, this division was formalized with the creation of two separate German states: the Federal Republic of Germany (West Germany), and the German Democratic Republic (East Germany).

For the people of Berlin, the division was particularly stark. The city, located deep within the Soviet zone of occupation, became a microcosm of the broader East-West conflict. The construction of the Berlin Wall in 1961 served as a physical manifestation of this division, sealing off East Berlin from the democratic enclave of West Berlin and symbolizing the stark ideological divide that had come to define the Cold War era.

But even as the Wall rose higher and the barriers grew more formidable, the desire for reunification remained strong among the German people. Families separated by the Wall communicated through letters and occasional visits, dreaming of the day when they would be reunited and the scars of division would be healed.

The division of Germany was more than just a geopolitical reality; it was a human tragedy, a testament to the enduring power of ideology to divide and conquer. But it was also a testament to the resilience of the human spirit, as ordinary men and women on both sides of the Wall dared to hope for a future free from the shadow of division and conflict.

Little did they know that their hopes would soon be realized in a moment of triumph and jubilation that would echo around the world. The fall of the Berlin Wall in 1989 would mark not just the reunification of a divided city, but the beginning of the end of the Cold War division that had divided Germany for four long decades.

The division of Germany after World War II didn't just delineate political boundaries; it etched profound scars on the psyche of the nation and its people. In the smoldering ruins of a defeated Reich, the Allied powers grappled with the daunting task of reshaping the European landscape amidst the looming specter of Soviet expansionism.

The division of Germany into East and USWest mirrored the broader ideological chasm that cleaved the world in two. West Germany, under the stewardship of the Western Allies, embarked on a path of democratic reconstruction, embracing the principles of freedom and free-market capitalism. In contrast, East Germany fell under the sway of the Soviet Union, becoming a puppet state beholden to Moscow's authoritarian regime.

For the people of Germany, the division was not just a geopolitical reality; it was a rupture that severed ties of kinship and tore apart the fabric of society. Families found themselves divided by barbed wire and armed guards, their reunions relegated to fleeting moments of joy amidst a backdrop of perpetual separation.

Nowhere was the division more starkly felt than in Berlin, a city cleaved in two by the cruel exigencies of history. The construction of the Berlin Wall in 1961 symbolized the entrenchment of this division, transforming the once-proud capital into a fortress of oppression and a potent symbol of Cold War confrontation.

But even in the shadow of the Wall, the yearning for unity burned bright in the hearts of Germans on both sides of the divide. From the bustling streets of West Berlin to the drab apartment blocks of East Berlin, the desire for reunification simmered just beneath the surface, waiting for the right moment to burst forth with irresistible force.

And burst forth it did, in a cacophony of joy and jubilation that reverberated around the world. The fall of the Berlin Wall in 1989 was more than just the crumbling of concrete and mortar; it was the shattering of the ideological barriers that had divided Germany for so long. In its wake came the heady rush of freedom and the promise of a brighter future, as East and West embraced each other as long-lost siblings reunited at last.

The division of Germany may have been a chapter in history, but its legacy endures as a testament to the resilience of the human spirit and the power of unity to overcome even the most formidable of obstacles. As we delve deeper into the story of the fall of the Berlin Wall, we will uncover the untold tales of courage, sacrifice, and hope that paved the way for this momentous event, reminding us that even in the darkest of times, the light of freedom can never be extinguished.

Chapter Two

Construction of the Berlin wall

The construction of the Berlin Wall stands as a somber milestone in the history of division and oppression that gripped Germany during the Cold War era. It was a physical manifestation of the ideological fault lines that cleaved East and West, a stark reminder of the lengths to which authoritarian regimes would go to maintain their grip on power.

The seeds of the Berlin Wall were sown in the years following World War II, as the Soviet Union solidified its control over Eastern Europe and tensions with the Western Allies escalated. By 1961, Berlin had become a hotbed of Cold War intrigue, a city divided not just by ideology, but by concrete barriers and armed checkpoints.

The decision to erect the Wall came as a shock to many, both inside and outside of Germany. Overnight, families were torn asunder, communities were split in two, and the hopes of a generation were dashed against the cold, hard reality of division.

But for the leaders of East Germany, the Wall was more than just a barrier; it was a symbol of strength and resolve in the face of Western aggression. It was a means of stemming the tide of defections to the West, of tightening their grip on power, and of asserting their dominance over their erstwhile allies. The construction of the Wall was a monumental undertaking, requiring the coordination of thousands of workers and the deployment of military forces to secure the border. Overnight, streets were torn up, buildings demolished, and barbed wire fences erected, creating a no-man's-land of desolation and despair.

For the people of Berlin, the Wall represented not just physical separation, but the crushing weight of oppression and despair. Families were torn apart, dreams were shattered, and the promise of freedom seemed more distant than ever before.

But even in the shadow of the Wall, the flame of hope refused to be extinguished. From the bustling streets of West Berlin to the desolate wastelands of No Man's Land, the desire for freedom burned bright in the hearts of those who dared to dream of a better tomorrow.

And it was this flame of hope that would ultimately prove to be the Wall's undoing. For in the end, no barrier, however formidable, could withstand the irresistible force of the human spirit longing to be free.

The construction of the Berlin Wall in August 1961 marked a pivotal moment in the history of Germany, Europe, and the Cold War. It was a physical manifestation of the deepening divide between East and West, a stark symbol of the ideological struggle that gripped the world in the aftermath of World War II.

The decision to build the Wall came amidst rising tensions between the Soviet Union and the Western Allies, particularly over the status of Berlin, which lay deep within the Soviet-controlled zone of East Germany. Faced with a steady stream of defections to the West, East German leader Walter Ulbricht sought a drastic solution to stem the exodus of skilled labor and intellectuals from his faltering regime.

Overnight, East German authorities began erecting barbed wire fences and concrete barriers along the border between East and West Berlin, effectively sealing off the eastern half of the city from the democratic enclave of the West. Families were torn apart, neighborhoods were divided, and the hopes of a generation were dashed against the cold, hard reality of division.

The construction of the Wall was a meticulously planned operation, coordinated by the East German government with the full backing of the Soviet Union. Thousands of soldiers and workers were deployed to the border, where they toiled day and night to erect the formidable barrier that would come to define Berlin for the next 28 years.

For the people of Berlin, the sudden appearance of the Wall was a profound shock, a brutal reminder of the fragility of freedom and the ruthlessness of authoritarian rule. Overnight, streets that had once bustled with life and activity were transformed into desolate no-man's-lands, patrolled by armed guards and overlooked by watchtowers.

But even in the face of such overwhelming oppression, the spirit of resistance refused to be extinguished. From daring escapes over the Wall to acts of civil disobedience in the streets, the people of Berlin continued to defy the tyranny of the Wall and the regime that had erected it.

And it was this spirit of defiance that would ultimately prove to be the Wall's downfall. For as the years passed and the winds of change swept across Eastern Europe, the cracks in the Wall grew wider and wider, until finally, on a crisp November night in 1989, the people of Berlin rose up as one and tore down the barrier that had divided them for so long.

The construction of the Berlin Wall may have been a dark chapter in the history of Germany, but it was also a testament to the power of the human spirit to resist oppression and defy tyranny. And as we reflect on this pivotal moment in history, we are reminded that even in the darkest of times, the flame of freedom burns eternal, lighting the way to a brighter tomorrow.

The construction of the Berlin Wall stands as a poignant symbol of the division and oppression that gripped Germany during the Cold War era. It was a physical barrier that not only separated families and communities but also symbolized the deep ideological chasm between East and West.

The decision to build the Wall was a drastic response to the growing crisis of defections from East to West Berlin. As East Germany struggled to retain its population and prevent the exodus of skilled workers and intellectuals, its leaders, under the guidance of the Soviet Union, saw the construction of a physical barrier as the only solution.

The suddenness of the Wall's construction caught many by surprise. Overnight, streets were torn up, buildings demolished, and barbed wire fences erected, creating a fortified border that sliced through the heart of Berlin. Families found themselves separated, their hopes of reunion dashed against the cold concrete and steel of the Wall.

But the Wall was more than just a physical barrier; it was a potent symbol of the broader East-West conflict that defined the Cold War era. It represented the stark divide between communism and capitalism, between freedom and oppression, that had plunged the world into a state of perpetual tension.

For the people of Berlin, the construction of the Wall was a devastating blow, a stark reminder of the fragility of freedom and the ever-present threat of totalitarianism. Overnight, they found themselves living in a city torn apart by barbed wire and armed guards, their dreams of unity and reconciliation shattered by the harsh realities of division.

But even in the face of such adversity, the spirit of resistance endured. From daring escapes over the Wall to acts of protest and defiance in the streets, the people of Berlin refused to accept the Wall as a permanent fixture of their lives. They continued to hope for a day when the barriers would come down and the city would be reunited once more.

And that day finally came on November 9, 1989, when the Wall was breached by a tide of jubilant East and West Berliners, who came together in a spirit of unity and reconciliation to tear down the barriers that had divided them for so long.

The construction of the Berlin Wall may have been a dark chapter in the history of Germany, but it was also a testament to the resilience of the human spirit and the power of hope to overcome even the most formidable of obstacles. And as we reflect on this pivotal moment in history, we are reminded that the walls we build between us are ultimately no match for the bonds of friendship, solidarity, and love that unite us as one human family.

Chapter three

Life In Divided Berlin

Life in divided Berlin was a tale of two cities, each existing in stark contrast to the other, yet bound together by the shared experience of living in the shadow of the Berlin Wall. For residents of West Berlin, life was characterized by freedom, prosperity, and the vibrant energy of a city that refused to be cowed by the specter of communism looming just beyond its borders.

In West Berlin, the streets hummed with activity, the cafes buzzed with conversation, and the nightlife pulsed with the rhythm of a city that knew how to live life to the fullest. Despite the constant reminder of the Wall that encircled their enclave, West Berliners embraced their status as an island of democracy in a sea of oppression, defiantly asserting their right to live free from the constraints of totalitarian rule.

But just across the Wall lay a very different reality. In East Berlin, life was characterized by scarcity, repression, and the omnipresent fear of the state. The East German regime, under the watchful eye of the Soviet Union, maintained tight control over every aspect of daily life, from the media and education to the arts and culture.

For East Berliners, the Wall was not just a physical barrier; it was a constant reminder of their status as second-class citizens in their own country. Families were torn apart, friendships severed, and dreams of a better life dashed against the cold, hard reality of communist rule.

Yet even in the face of such adversity, the people of East Berlin found ways to resist and endure. From underground dissident movements to acts of quiet defiance in their everyday lives, they refused to be cowed by the oppressive regime that sought to crush their spirit.

And amidst the darkness of division, there were moments of light. Families reunited across the Wall, lovers rendezvoused in secret, and friendships flourished in the face of adversity. Despite the best efforts of the East German regime to divide and conquer, the bonds of humanity proved stronger than the barriers of concrete and barbed wire.

The story of life in divided Berlin is a testament to the resilience of the human spirit and the enduring power of hope in the face of adversity. It is a reminder that even in the darkest of times, the flame of freedom can never be extinguished, and that the bonds of friendship and solidarity can transcend even the most formidable of barriers.

Life in divided Berlin was a paradoxical existence, where the vibrancy of one side stood in stark contrast to the oppression of the other. In West Berlin, residents enjoyed the fruits of democracy and capitalism, living in a bustling metropolis that served as a beacon of freedom in the heart of Cold War Europe.

For West Berliners, the Wall was a constant reminder of the precariousness of their situation, yet it also served as a symbol of their resilience and determination to defy the forces of tyranny. Despite the physical barriers and the ever-present threat of communist incursion, West Berlin thrived as a cultural and economic powerhouse, attracting artists, intellectuals, and entrepreneurs from around the world.

But just a stone's throw away lay a very different reality. In East Berlin, life was characterized by scarcity, surveillance, and the suffocating grip of the state. The East German regime, under the watchful eye of the Soviet Union, imposed strict controls on every aspect of daily life, from the media and education to religion and dissent.

For East Berliners, the Wall was more than just a physical barrier; it was a psychological barrier that divided families, fractured communities, and stifled the aspirations of an entire generation. Yet even in the face of such oppression, the human spirit refused to be extinguished.

From clandestine meetings in dimly lit apartments to whispered conversations in smoky cafes, East Berliners found ways to resist the oppressive regime that sought to crush their spirit. Despite the ever-present threat of arrest, imprisonment, or worse, they continued to hold onto their dreams of freedom and democracy, refusing to accept the Wall as the final word on their fate.

And amidst the darkness of division, there were moments of light. Families reunited across the Wall, lovers stole moments of intimacy in the shadows, and friends found solace in each other's company. Despite the best efforts of the authorities to sow fear and division, the bonds of humanity proved stronger than the barriers of concrete and steel.

The story of life in divided Berlin is a testament to the resilience of the human spirit and the enduring power of hope in the face of adversity. It is a reminder that even in the darkest of times, the flame of freedom can never be extinguished, and that the bonds of friendship and solidarity can transcend even the most formidable of barriers.

Living in divided Berlin was akin to inhabiting two different worlds within the confines of one city. On the western side of the Wall, life pulsated with the energy of freedom and opportunity. West Berlin, an island of democracy in the midst of a sea of communist rule, thrived as a vibrant cultural hub, attracting artists, intellectuals, and entrepreneurs from across the globe.

In West Berlin, the streets teemed with life, lined with cafes, theaters, and galleries where ideas flowed freely and creativity knew no bounds. Despite the looming presence of the Wall, West Berliners embraced their status as citizens of a free and open society, reveling in their ability to live life on their own terms.

But just a stone's throw away lay a very different reality. In East Berlin, life was a study in contrasts – a landscape of drab conformity and state-sanctioned oppression. The East German regime, under the watchful eye of the Soviet Union, imposed strict controls on every aspect of daily life, from the media and education to employment and travel.

For East Berliners, the Wall was more than just a physical barrier; it was a constant reminder of their status as prisoners in their own city. Families were torn apart, friendships severed, and dreams of a better future crushed beneath the weight of communist rule.

Yet even in the face of such adversity, the human spirit persevered. From clandestine gatherings in cramped apartments to acts of quiet defiance on the streets, East Berliners found ways to resist the suffocating embrace of the regime. They clung to the hope that one day the barriers would come down, and they would be free to live their lives without fear or oppression.

And amidst the darkness of division, there were moments of light. Families reunited across the Wall, lovers stole fleeting moments of intimacy in the shadows, and friends found solace in each other's company. Despite the best efforts of the authorities to sow fear and division, the bonds of humanity proved stronger than the barriers of concrete and barbed wire.

The story of life in divided Berlin is a testament to the resilience of the human spirit and the enduring power of hope in the face of adversity. It is a reminder that even in the darkest of times, the flame of freedom can never be extinguished, and that the bonds of friendship and solidarity can transcend even the most formidable of barriers.

Chapter four

Evolving International Relationship

The division of Berlin was not just a local issue; it was a flashpoint in the broader context of international relations during the Cold War era. The construction of the Berlin Wall in 1961 served as a stark reminder of the deepening divide between East and West, and its impact rippled far beyond the borders of Germany.

At the heart of the division lay the ideological struggle between communism and capitalism, between the Soviet Union and the United States, which had defined global politics since the end of World War II. Berlin, situated deep within the Soviet-controlled zone of East Germany, became a microcosm of this larger conflict, a city divided not just by physical barriers, but by competing visions of the future.

The construction of the Berlin Wall sent shockwaves through the international community, raising fears of a potential military confrontation between the superpowers. The United States and its Western allies condemned the Wall as a symbol of oppression and tyranny, while the Soviet Union and its allies defended it as a necessary measure to protect the socialist experiment from Western subversion.

Yet even as tensions escalated, diplomatic channels remained open, as both sides recognized the dangers of allowing the situation in Berlin to spiral out of control. The Cuban Missile Crisis of 1962, which brought the world to the brink of nuclear war, served as a stark reminder of the stakes involved in the East-West rivalry.

As the years passed, however, a gradual thaw began to take hold in East-West relations, driven in part by changing leadership in both the United States and the Soviet Union. The policies of détente pursued by Presidents Nixon and Brezhnev sought to ease tensions and promote dialogue between the superpowers, paving the way for a series of arms control agreements and cultural exchanges.

Meanwhile, events in Eastern Europe, such as the rise of the Solidarity movement in Poland and the election of reform-minded leaders in Hungary and Czechoslovakia, signaled a growing desire for change among the populations of the Soviet bloc. The Soviet Union, under the leadership of Mikhail Gorbachev, embarked on a program of reform known as perestroika, which sought to revitalize the stagnant Soviet economy and promote greater openness and transparency in government.

These developments set the stage for the dramatic events of 1989, when a wave of peaceful revolutions swept across Eastern Europe, toppling communist regimes and paving the way for the reunification of Germany. The fall of the Berlin Wall on November 9, 1989, symbolized not just the end of a physical barrier, but the beginning of a new era in international relations, characterized by greater cooperation and dialogue between East and West.

The evolving international relations surrounding the division of Berlin remind us that even in the midst of seemingly intractable conflicts, there is always room for dialogue and diplomacy. It is a testament to the power of engagement and negotiation to overcome even the most entrenched divisions and build a more peaceful and prosperous world for future generation

The division of Berlin was a microcosm of the broader geopolitical struggle between the superpowers during the Cold War era. As the Wall rose in 1961, it became a potent symbol of the deepening divide between East and West, sparking fears of a potential military confrontation that could escalate into a global conflict.

The United States and its Western allies viewed the construction of the Wall as a brazen act of aggression by the Soviet Union and its satellite states in Eastern Europe. They condemned it as a flagrant violation of human rights and a stark reminder of the dangers posed by communist expansionism.

In response, the Western powers reaffirmed their commitment to defending the freedom and security of West Berlin, pledging to maintain a military presence in the city and provide economic and diplomatic support to its embattled residents. The creation of NATO and the deployment of American troops to Europe served as a visible demonstration of Western resolve in the face of Soviet aggression. For the Soviet Union and its allies, the construction of the Wall was a defensive measure aimed at safeguarding the gains of the socialist revolution from Western encroachment. They portrayed it as a necessary response to Western provocations and a means of protecting the socialist experiment from the corrosive influence of capitalism.

Despite the escalating tensions, however, both sides recognized the dangers of allowing the situation in Berlin to spiral out of control. Backchannel communications and diplomatic channels remalned open, as both sides sought to avoid a direct confrontation that could lead to catastrophic consequences for the entire world.

The Cuban Missile Crisis of 1962, which brought the United States and the Soviet Union to the brink of nuclear war, served as a sobering reminder of the dangers of allowing Cold War rivalries to escalate unchecked. It prompted a renewed commitment to dialogue and negotiation, as both sides sought to find ways to manage their differences and prevent a repeat of the crisis.

As the years passed, a gradual thaw began to take hold in East-West relations, driven in part by changing leadership and shifting geopolitical realities. The policies of détente pursued by Presidents Nixon and Brezhnev sought to ease tensions and promote dialogue between the superpowers, paving the way for a series of arms control agreements and cultural exchanges.

Meanwhile, events in Eastern Europe, such as the rise of dissident movements and the election of reform-minded leaders, signaled a growing desire for change among the populations of the Soviet bloc. The Soviet Union, under the leadership of Mikhail Gorbachev, embarked on a program of reform known as perestroika, which sought to revitalize the stagnant Soviet economy and promote greater openness and transparency in government.

These developments set the stage for the dramatic events of 1989, when a wave of peaceful revolutions swept across Eastern Europe, toppling communist regimes and paving the way for the reunification of Germany. The fall of the Berlin Wall on November 9, 1989, symbolized not just the end of a physical barrier, but the beginning of a new era in international relations, characterized by greater cooperation and dialogue between East and West.

The evolving international relations surrounding the division of Berlin remind us that even in the midst of seemingly intractable conflicts, there is always room for dialogue and diplomacy. It is a testament to the power of engagement and negotiation to overcome even the most entrenched divisions and build a more peaceful and prosperous world for future generations.

Chapter five

Protest And Dissent

The division of Berlin ignited a wave of protests and dissent that reverberated both within the city and across the globe. From the moment the Wall was erected in 1961, Berliners on both sides of the divide refused to accept the status quo, challenging the oppressive regime that sought to keep them apart.

In West Berlin, protests took on a more vocal and visible form, as residents of the enclave defiantly asserted their right to live free from the constraints of communism. From rallies and demonstrations to acts of civil disobedience, West Berliners made their voices heard, demanding an end to the division that cleaved their city in two.

But perhaps the most iconic symbol of protest in West Berlin was the annual Berlin Wall graffiti protest. Every year, on the anniversary of the Wall's construction, artists and activists from around the world descended on the city to paint messages of peace, unity, and defiance on the concrete barrier that divided East and West.

In East Berlin, dissent took on a more clandestine and subversive form, as residents of the communist enclave risked arrest, imprisonment, and even death to defy the regime that sought to control every aspect of their lives. Underground dissident movements sprang up, spreading messages of resistance through leaflets, pamphlets, and secret meetings.

But perhaps the most powerful form of dissent in East Berlin was the act of escaping across the Wall to the West. Despite the ever-present threat of gunfire, barbed wire, and armed guards, thousands of East Berliners risked their lives in daring attempts to breach the barrier that separated them from freedom.

The most famous of these escapes occurred on August 17, 1962, when 18-year-old Peter Fechter was shot and killed by East German border guards as he attempted to flee to the West. His death became a symbol of the brutality of the regime and the lengths to which its leaders would go to maintain their grip on power.

Yet even in the face of such repression, the flame of dissent refused to be extinguished. From the streets of West Berlin to the shadows of East Berlin, the people of the divided city continued to resist, to protest, and to dream of a day when the barriers would come down and the city would be reunited once more.

And it was this spirit of defiance that would ultimately prove to be the Wall's downfall. For in the end, no barrier, however formidable, could withstand the irresistible force of the human spirit longing to be free.

The construction of the Berlin Wall in 1961 sparked a wave of protests and dissent that echoed throughout the divided city and reverberated across the globe. From the moment the Wall rose, Berliners on both sides of the divide refused to accept the arbitrary separation imposed upon them by the ruling regimes.

In West Berlin, where the ideals of freedom and democracy were cherished, protests took on a vocal and public form. Citizens gathered in the streets, holding rallies, and demonstrations, demanding an end to the division that tore their city apart. They painted messages of solidarity and defiance on the western side of the Wall, turning it into a canvas for their hopes and dreams of reunification.

The annual Berlin Wall graffiti protest became a powerful symbol of resistance, drawing artists and activists from around the world to leave their mark on the concrete barrier that symbolized oppression and tyranny. Each stroke of paint was a testament to the indomitable human spirit and a declaration of solidarity with those trapped behind the Iron Curtain.

In East Berlin, dissent took on a more clandestine and dangerous form. Underground dissident movements sprang up, spreading messages of resistance through secret meetings and samizdat publications. Brave individuals risked arrest, imprisonment, and even death to speak out against the oppressive regime and demand their rights to freedom and self-determination.

The act of escaping across the Wall became the ultimate form of dissent for many East Berliners. Despite the ever-present danger of gunfire and barbed wire, thousands attempted daring escapes, determined to reclaim their freedom and reunite with loved ones on the other side. Each successful escape was a victory against tyranny and a testament to the resilience of the human spirit.

But for every successful escape, there were countless others that ended in tragedy. The deaths of those who perished while attempting to breach the Wall served as a stark reminder of the brutality of the regime and the lengths to which it would go to maintain its grip on power.

Yet even in the face of such repression and violence, the spirit of dissent persisted. From the streets of West Berlin to the shadows of East Berlin, the people of the divided city continued to resist, to protest, and to dream of a day when the barriers would come down and the city would be reunited once more.

And it was this spirit of defiance that would ultimately prove to be the Wall's downfall. For in the end, no barrier, however formidable, could withstand the overwhelming tide of human longing for freedom and justice.

side. Each successful escape was a victory against tyranny and a testament to the resilience of the human spirit.

But for every successful escape, there were countless others that ended in tragedy. The deaths of those who perished while attempting to breach the Wall served as a stark reminder of the brutality of the regime and the lengths to which it would go to maintain its grip on power.

Yet even in the face of such repression and violence, the spirit of dissent persisted. From the streets of West Berlin to the shadows of East Berlin, the people of the divided city continued to resist, to protest, and to dream of a day when the barriers would come down and the city would be reunited once more.

And it was this spirit of defiance that would ultimately prove to be the Wall's downfall. For in the end, no barrier, however formidable, could withstand the overwhelming tide of human longing for freedom and justice.

Chapter six

Gorbachev and Perestroika

Amidst the backdrop of protests and dissent in Berlin and across Eastern Europe, a new leader emerged in the Soviet Union whose policies would have profound implications for the future of the Cold War and the division of Berlin. Mikhail Gorbachev, the youthful and reform-minded General Secretary of the Communist Party, came to power in 1985 with a vision of revitalizing the stagnant Soviet economy and promoting greater openness and transparency in government.

Gorbachev's policies, collectively known as perestroika, sought to modernize the Soviet economy by introducing elements of market competition and private enterprise, while also promoting greater political liberalization and democratization. His bold reforms represented a departure from the hardline policies of his predecessors and signaled a willingness to engage with the West in pursuit of a more stable and prosperous world order.

The impact of perestroika was felt far beyond the borders of the Soviet Union, as Eastern European countries, including East Germany, began to clamor for greater autonomy and reform. The winds of change sweeping through the region emboldened dissident movements and fueled demands for political reform, economic restructuring, and greater respect for human rights.

In East Berlin, Gorbachev's policies were met with a mixture of hope and trepidation. While many welcomed the prospect of greater openness and reform, others feared that the changes sweeping through the region could destabilize the status quo and threaten the grip of the ruling regime.

But Gorbachev's commitment to reform remained steadfast, even in the face of resistance from hardline elements within the Communist Party. His insistence on greater transparency and accountability in government, coupled with his willingness to engage in dialogue with the West, set the stage for a historic transformation in East-West relations.

As the Cold War entered its final years, Gorbachev's efforts to promote détente and reduce tensions with the West paved the way for a series of breakthrough agreements, including the Intermediate-Range Nuclear Forces (INF) Treaty and the Strategic Arms Reduction Treaty (START). These agreements helped to ease fears of a nuclear confrontation and laid the groundwork for greater cooperation between East and West.

But perhaps Gorbachev's most enduring legacy was his role in facilitating the peaceful revolutions that swept across Eastern Europe in 1989, toppling communist regimes and paving the way for the reunification of Germany. His decision not to intervene militarily in response to the protests and dissent that erupted in Berlin and elsewhere was a courageous act that helped to avert a potential catastrophe and set the stage for a new era of cooperation and reconciliation in Europe.

Gorbachev's leadership and the reforms of perestroika played a decisive role in bringing an end to the division of Berlin and the broader Cold War division that had divided Europe for nearly half a century. His vision of a more open, democratic, and peaceful world order continues to inspire generations of leaders and activists striving to build a better future for all.

:

Amidst the tumultuous events unfolding in Berlin and across Eastern Europe, the emergence of Mikhail Gorbachev as the leader of the Soviet Union marked a turning point in the Cold War dynamic. Gorbachev's ascension to power in 1985 brought with it a breath of fresh air, as he embarked on a mission to reform the stagnant Soviet economy and revitalize the country's political landscape through his policies of perestroika and glasnost.

Perestroika, meaning "restructuring," aimed to modernize the Soviet economy by introducing elements of market competition and private enterprise. Gorbachev recognized the inefficiencies and stagnation that had plagued the Soviet system for decades and sought to inject new life into the economy through decentralization and greater autonomy for state enterprises.

But perestroika was not just about economic reform; it was also a call for greater political openness and transparency. Gorbachev's policy of glasnost, or "openness," encouraged greater freedom of speech, press, and assembly, allowing for a more vibrant public discourse and a more engaged citizenry.

The impact of Gorbachev's reforms was felt far beyond the borders of the Soviet Union, as the winds of change swept through Eastern Europe, fueling demands for political reform and greater autonomy from the communist regimes that ruled the region. In East Germany, the policies of perestroika emboldened dissident movements and fueled calls for greater freedom and democracy.

But Gorbachev's commitment to reform was not without its challenges. Hardline elements within the Communist Party resisted his efforts to liberalize the Soviet system, fearing that greater openness would lead to the unraveling of the socialist experiment. And as protests and dissent spread across Eastern Europe, Gorbachev found himself walking a fine line between supporting the aspirations of the people and maintaining stability within the Soviet bloc.

Yet despite these challenges, Gorbachev remained steadfast in his commitment to reform and détente with the West. His willingness to engage in dialogue with Western leaders and negotiate arms control agreements helped to ease tensions between East and West, paving the way for a more stable and cooperative relationship between the superpowers.

Ultimately, Gorbachev's reforms and his willingness to embrace change played a decisive role in bringing an end to the division of Berlin and the broader Cold War division that had divided Europe for decades. His vision of a more open, democratic, and peaceful world order continues to inspire leaders and activists around the globe, reminding us that even in the darkest of times, the human spirit has the power to overcome adversity and build a brighter future for all.

Chapter seven

Hungary and the Pan-European Picnic

In the summer of 1989, against the backdrop of sweeping political changes and growing calls for reform across Eastern Europe, Hungary played a pivotal role in hastening the collapse of the Iron Curtain and the division of Berlin. The Pan-European Picnic, held on August 19th near the Austrian-Hungarian border, served as a catalyst for the events that would ultimately lead to the fall of the Berlin Wall.

The Pan-European Picnic was conceived as a symbolic gesture of unity and solidarity, aimed at highlighting the artificial barriers that divided Europe and promoting greater cooperation and understanding between East and West. Organized by activists from Hungary and Austria, the event attracted thousands of participants from both sides of the Iron Curtain, who gathered together to enjoy music, food, and cultural performances in a spirit of camaraderie and friendship.

But the Picnic took on a significance far beyond its organizers' intentions when hundreds of East Germans seized the opportunity to escape to the West. Faced with the prospect of being caught up in a mass exodus, Hungarian border guards made the fateful decision to open the border, allowing the refugees to cross into Austria and freedom.

The scenes of jubilation and relief that followed sent shockwaves throughout Eastern Europe and served as a powerful symbol of the growing desire for change and freedom that was sweeping the region. The Pan-European Picnic had inadvertently become a turning point in the struggle against communist rule, igniting a chain reaction of protests and dissent that would ultimately lead to the collapse of the Berlin Wall and the reunification of Germany.

The events of the Pan-European Picnic demonstrated the power of people to overcome the barriers of division and oppression through peaceful means. They showed that even in the face of seemingly insurmountable obstacles, the human spirit longs for freedom and will seize any opportunity to break free from the shackles of tyranny.

In the years since the Pan-European Picnic, Hungary has continued to play a central role in shaping the future of Europe, embracing democracy, and joining the European Union. The legacy of the Picnic serves as a reminder of the importance of unity, cooperation, and solidarity in the pursuit of a more peaceful and prosperous world for all.

In the summer of 1989, Hungary found itself at the epicenter of a seismic shift in European history, as the Pan-European Picnic unfolded near the border with Austria. This seemingly innocuous event, organized by activists from Hungary and Austria, quickly escalated into a pivotal moment that would hasten the demise of the Iron Curtain and the division of Berlin.

The Pan-European Picnic was conceived as a symbolic gesture of unity and solidarity, aimed at highlighting the artificial barriers that divided Europe and promoting greater cooperation and understanding between East and West. Thousands of people from both sides of the Iron Curtain flocked to the event, drawn by the promise of music, food, and cultural exchange.

But what began as a celebration of friendship and camaraderie soon took on a more serious tone when hundreds of East Germans seized the opportunity to escape to the West. Faced with the prospect of being caught up in a mass exodus,

Hungarian border guards made the momentous decision to open the border, allowing the refugees to cross into Austria and freedom.

The scenes of joy and relief that followed sent shockwaves throughout Eastern Europe and served as a powerful symbol of the growing desire for change and freedom that was sweeping the region. The Pan-European Picnic had inadvertently become a catalyst for the events that would ultimately lead to the fall of the Berlin Wall and the reunification of Germany.

For Hungary, the decision to open its borders was not without risks. The ruling Communist regime faced pressure from hardliners within the party who opposed any hint of liberalization or reform. But the events of the Pan-European Picnic forced the government's hand, revealing the deep-seated desire for change among the Hungarian people and the futility of trying to cling to the status quo in the face of overwhelming popular demand.

In the years since the Pan-European Picnic, Hungary has undergone a remarkable transformation, embracing democracy, and joining the European Union. The legacy of the Picnic serves as a reminder of the power of ordinary people to effect change and overcome the barriers of division and oppression through peaceful means.

As Hungary looks to the future, the lessons of the Pan-European Picnic remain as relevant as ever. They remind us that even in the darkest of times, the human spirit longs for freedom and will seize any opportunity to break free from the shackles of tyranny. And they remind us that unity, cooperation, and solidarity are the keys to building a more peaceful and prosperous world for all.

Chapter eight

Mass Demonstrations

The summer of 1989 witnessed a groundswell of mass demonstrations across Eastern Europe, fueled by growing discontent with communist rule and inspired by the events unfolding in Hungary and the Pan-European Picnic. From Berlin to Budapest, Prague to Warsaw, ordinary citizens took to the streets to demand political reform, economic freedom, and an end to the divisions that had torn their continent apart for decades.

In East Germany, mass demonstrations erupted in cities and towns across the country, as thousands of people took to the streets to demand greater political freedom and an end to the oppressive regime that ruled over them. The protests gained momentum in the wake of the Pan-European Picnic, as East Germans saw the possibility of change on the horizon and seized the opportunity to make their voices heard.

In Leipzig, weekly demonstrations attracted hundreds of thousands of people, making them some of the largest protests in East German history. Despite the ever-present threat of violence from the authorities, the protesters remained defiant, refusing to back down until their demands for democracy and freedom were met.

In Prague, the Velvet Revolution brought hundreds of thousands of people into the streets, calling for an end to communist rule and the establishment of a democratic government. Led by dissident leaders such as Vaclav Havel, the protesters engaged in nonviolent resistance, staging sit-ins, strikes, and marches to pressure the regime into conceding to their demands.

In Warsaw, the Solidarity movement, led by Lech Walesa, led mass strikes and protests that brought the country to a standstill, forcing the ruling Communist Party to enter into negotiations with the opposition and ultimately paving the way for free elections and the end of communist rule in Poland.

But perhaps the most iconic of all the mass demonstrations of 1989 were those that took place in Berlin. In the months leading up to the fall of the Berlin Wall, hundreds of thousands of people took to the streets to demand an end to the division that had torn their city apart for nearly three decades. Their chants of "Wir sind das Volk" ("We are the people") echoed through the streets, a powerful reminder of the collective will of the people to reclaim their freedom and their right to determine their own destiny.

The mass demonstrations of 1989 were a testament to the power of ordinary people to effect change and overcome the barriers of division and oppression through peaceful means. They showed that even in the face of seemingly insurmountable odds, the human spirit longs for freedom and will stop at nothing to achieve it. And they serve as a reminder that unity, solidarity, and the courage to stand up for what is right are the keys to building a better future for all.

:

The summer of 1989 was a watershed moment in the history of Eastern Europe, as mass demonstrations swept across the region, challenging the grip of communist regimes and setting the stage for the collapse of the Berlin Wall and the reunification of Germany. From Leipzig to Prague, Warsaw to Budapest, ordinary citizens took to the streets to demand political reform, economic freedom, and an end to the divisions that had divided their continent for decades.

In East Germany, the weekly protests that began in Leipzig quickly spread to other cities and towns, swelling in size as more and more people joined the ranks of the demonstrators. Despite the ever-present threat of violence from the authorities, the protesters remained resolute, chanting slogans of "Wir sind das Volk" ("We are the people") and demanding an end to the repressive regime that ruled over them.

In Prague, the Velvet Revolution brought hundreds of thousands of people into the streets, as the people of Czechoslovakia demanded an end to communist rule and the establishment of a democratic government. Led by dissident leaders such as Vaclav Havel, the protesters engaged in nonviolent resistance, staging sit-ins, strikes, and marches to pressure the regime into conceding to their demands.

In Poland, the Solidarity movement led mass strikes and protests that brought the country to a standstill, forcing the ruling Communist Party to enter into negotiations with the opposition and ultimately paving the way for free elections and the end of communist rule.

But perhaps the most iconic of all the mass demonstrations of 1989 were those that took place in Berlin. In the months leading up to the fall of the Berlin Wall, hundreds of thousands of people took to the streets to demand an end to the division that had torn their city apart for nearly three decades. Their chants of "Wir sind das Volk" ("We are the people") echoed through the streets, a powerful reminder of the collective will of the people to reclaim their freedom and their right to determine their own destiny.

The mass demonstrations of 1989 were a testament to the power of ordinary people to effect change and overcome the barriers of division and oppression through peaceful means. They showed that even in the face of seemingly insurmountable odds, the human spirit longs for freedom and will stop at nothing to achieve it. And they serve as a reminder that unity, solidarity, and the courage to stand up for what is right are the keys to building a better future for all.

Chapter nine

The Fall Of The Berlin Wall

On the evening of November 9, 1989, the world watched in awe and disbelief as the Berlin Wall, the physical embodiment of the Cold War division between East and West, finally crumbled. The fall of the Wall was the culmination of months of mass demonstrations, political upheaval, and grassroots activism that had swept across Eastern Europe, challenging the grip of communist regimes and demanding an end to the divisions that had separated families and communities for nearly three decades.

The events that led to the fall of the Berlin Wall were set in motion months earlier, as the winds of change swept through Eastern Europe, fueled by growing discontent with communist rule and inspired by the reforms of Mikhail Gorbachev in the Soviet Union. In Hungary, the Pan-European Picnic had inadvertently opened the floodgates, as hundreds of East Germans seized the opportunity to escape to the West, forcing the Hungarian government to open its borders and setting off a chain reaction of protests and dissent across the region.

In East Germany, the weekly demonstrations that began in Leipzig quickly spread to other cities and towns, swelling in size as more and more people joined the ranks of the demonstrators. The regime, faced with mounting pressure from both within and without, found itself increasingly isolated and incapable of stemming the tide of change.

And then, on that fateful evening in November, the unthinkable happened. In a moment of confusion and miscommunication, a government spokesman announced that East Germans would be allowed to travel freely to the West. Within hours, tens of thousands of people descended upon the Wall, armed with hammers and chisels, ready to tear down the hated symbol of oppression that had divided their city for so long.

As the world looked on in astonishment, the barriers that had separated East and West Berlin for nearly three decades came crashing down, and jubilant crowds surged across the once-impenetrable divide, embracing their long-lost friends and family members in tearful reunions. The fall of the Berlin Wall was not just the end of a physical barrier; it was the end of an era, a symbolic triumph of freedom over tyranny, and a testament to the power of ordinary people to effect change through peaceful means.

In the months and years that followed, the reunification of Germany and the end of the Cold War would usher in a new era of hope and optimism for millions of people around the world. But the memory of that historic night in November 1989 would remain etched in the collective consciousness as a reminder of the enduring power of the human spirit to overcome even the most formidable of obstacles in the pursuit of freedom and justice.

The fall of the Berlin Wall on November 9, 1989, stands as one of the most iconic moments of the 20th century, symbolizing the end of an era defined by division and repression and marking the beginning of a new era of hope and unity for Germany and the world.

For nearly three decades, the Berlin Wall had stood as a physical and ideological barrier, dividing the city of Berlin and symbolizing the deep-seated divisions between East and West in the Cold War era. It was a stark reminder of the bitter rivalries and tensions that had defined international relations since the end of World War II.

But on that historic night in November, the Wall became a symbol not of division, but of unity and liberation, as thousands of East Berliners poured across the once-impenetrable barrier to embrace their fellow citizens in the West. The scenes of joy and celebration that followed were a testament to the resilience of the human spirit and the yearning for freedom that had long been suppressed under communist rule.

The fall of the Berlin Wall was not just a spontaneous outburst of emotion; it was the culmination of months of mass demonstrations, political upheaval, and grassroots activism that had swept across Eastern Europe, challenging the authority of communist regimes and demanding an end to the divisions that had separated families and communities for generations.

In East Germany, the weekly protests that began in Leipzig quickly spread to other cities and towns, as ordinary citizens took to the streets to demand greater political freedom and an end to the repressive regime that ruled over them. The regime, faced with mounting pressure from both within and without, found itself increasingly isolated and incapable of stemming the tide of change.

The fall of the Berlin Wall sent shockwaves throughout the world, as people everywhere watched in awe and disbelief as the seemingly impossible became reality. It was a moment of triumph for democracy and human rights, and a stark reminder of the power of ordinary people to effect change through peaceful means.

In the months and years that followed, the reunification of Germany and the end of the Cold War would usher in a new era of hope and optimism for millions of people around the world. But the memory of that historic night in November 1989 would remain etched in the collective consciousness as a reminder of the enduring power of the human spirit to overcome even the most formidable of obstacles in the pursuit of freedom and justice.

Chapter ten

Aftermath And Reunification

The fall of the Berlin Wall on November 9, 1989, marked the beginning of a new chapter in German history, as the long-divided nation embarked on the path to reunification and reconciliation. In the weeks and months that followed, the people of East and West Germany grappled with the challenges and opportunities that lay ahead, as they sought to overcome decades of division and build a united and prosperous nation.

For East Germans, the fall of the Wall brought both joy and uncertainty. While many celebrated the end of communist rule and the prospect of reunification with their fellow countrymen in the West, others feared the economic and social upheaval that would accompany the transition to a market-based economy and the integration of the two Germanys.

In West Germany, the prospect of reunification was met with both excitement and trepidation. While many welcomed the opportunity to reunite with their long-lost brethren in the East and to rebuild a united Germany based on the principles of democracy and freedom, others worried about the economic and logistical challenges of integrating the two economies and societies.

But despite the challenges, the people of Germany were determined to overcome the obstacles that lay in their path and to build a brighter future for themselves and their children. In December 1989, just weeks after the fall of the Wall, the leaders of East and West Germany signed the Treaty of Reunification, paving the way for the formal reunification of the two Germanys on October 3, 1990.

The reunification of Germany was a momentous occasion, as East and West came together to celebrate the end of division and the beginning of a new era of unity and cooperation. But the process of reunification was not without its difficulties, as the two Germanys grappled with the economic, social, and political challenges of integration.

In the years that followed, Germany underwent a period of rapid transformation and reconstruction, as the people of East and West worked together to rebuild their country and to forge a new national identity. Despite the inevitable challenges and setbacks, the reunification of Germany stands as a testament to the resilience of the human spirit and the power of unity to overcome even the most formidable of obstacles.

Today, Germany stands as a shining example of what can be achieved when people come together in pursuit of a common goal. The reunification of Germany serves as a reminder of the enduring power of hope and optimism to overcome division and adversity and to build a better future for all.

The fall of the Berlin Wall unleashed a whirlwind of emotions and aspirations, as East and West Germany grappled with the aftermath of decades of division and the prospects of reunification. While the euphoria of freedom and unity swept through the hearts of Germans on both sides, the road to reunification was fraught with challenges, uncertainties, and poignant moments of reconciliation.

For East Germans, the collapse of the Wall represented the dawning of a new era of possibilities. The lifting of travel restrictions and the prospect of reunification brought both excitement and trepidation. While many yearned for the economic opportunities and personal freedoms enjoyed in the West, others grappled with the loss of the familiar comforts and certainties of their socialist existence.

In West Germany, the reunification of the country was met with a mixture of jubilation and apprehension. While there was a deep sense of pride in the prospect of reuniting with fellow Germans in the East and overcoming the scars of division, there were also concerns about the economic and social costs of integration.

The process of reunification was a complex and multifaceted endeavor that required careful negotiation and compromise on both sides. Economic disparities between East and West posed significant challenges, as East Germany struggled to adapt to the realities of a market economy and Western standards of living. The transfer of wealth and resources from West to East, while necessary for the rebuilding of the former communist state, strained the budgets and patience of West German taxpayers.

Socially, the reunification of Germany presented its own set of challenges, as East and West Germans confronted the legacy of four decades of separation and the divergent experiences of life under different political systems. Cultural differences, linguistic nuances, and ideological divisions served as barriers to integration, even as Germans on both sides sought to bridge the gap and forge a new national identity.

Despite the challenges, the reunification of Germany was ultimately a triumph of the human spirit and a testament to the power of unity and perseverance. On October 3, 1990, East and West Germany officially became one nation again, as the German Democratic Republic ceased to exist and the Federal Republic of Germany expanded to encompass the territory of the former East.

The reunification of Germany was a moment of celebration and reflection, as Germans from all walks of life came together to commemorate the end of division and the beginning of a new chapter in their nation's history. It was a time of hope and optimism, as East and West Germans looked forward to building a brighter future together, based on the principles of democracy, freedom, and unity.

Conclusion

As we reach the culmination of this incredible journey through the history of the fall of the Berlin Wall and the reunification of Germany, one thing becomes abundantly clear: this is not just a story of political intrigue or geopolitical maneuvering. It is a story of resilience, of hope, and of the indomitable human spirit overcoming seemingly insurmountable obstacles to achieve the impossible.

From the dramatic events that unfolded on that fateful night in November 1989, when the Berlin Wall crumbled beneath the weight of the people's desire for freedom, to the painstaking process of reunification that followed, every page of this saga is filled with moments of triumph and tragedy, of joy and sorrow, of courage and determination.

But beyond the historical significance and political ramifications, this is a story of ordinary people doing extraordinary things. It is a story of the East Berliners who risked everything to escape to the West, of the West Berliners who stood in solidarity with their neighbors across the Wall, and of the countless individuals on both sides who dared to dream of a better future for themselves and their children.

As you turn the final pages of this book, I urge you to reflect on the lessons of the past and to draw inspiration from the courage and resilience of those who came before us. For in their stories lies the blueprint for building a better world, where walls are torn down instead of built up, where divisions are bridged instead of deepened, and where the human spirit is free to soar to new heights of possibility and potential.

So, dear reader, I invite you to join me on this remarkable journey through history, as we explore the untold stories and hidden truths behind one of the most pivotal moments of the 20th century. For in the pages of this book, you will find not just a chronicle of events, but a testament to the enduring power of hope, of unity, and of the human spirit to triumph over adversity and to forge a brighter future for all.

As we come to the end of our exploration into the fall of the Berlin Wall and the subsequent reunification of Germany, we find ourselves not merely witnesses to history, but participants in a transformative journey that continues to shape the world we live in today.

The saga of the Berlin Wall is more than just a tale of political upheaval; it is a testament to the resilience of the human spirit and the power of unity to overcome division and oppression. It is a reminder that even in the darkest of times, hope can flourish, and change can be achieved through the collective will of ordinary people.

The fall of the Berlin Wall was a moment of profound significance, not only for Germany but for the entire world. It marked the end of an era defined by ideological conflict and the beginning of a new era of cooperation and reconciliation. It shattered the illusions of permanence and inevitability that had surrounded the Wall for so long and proved that even the most formidable barriers can be overcome when people come together in pursuit of a common goal.

But the story does not end with the fall of the Wall; it continues to unfold in the years and decades that follow. The reunification of Germany was a monumental achievement, but it also brought with it new challenges and opportunities. As East and West Germany embarked on the path of integration, they faced questions of identity, economy, and governance that would shape the future of the nation for generations to come.

Today, as we look back on the events of 1989 with the benefit of hindsight, we are reminded of the importance of remembering the lessons of the past. The fall of the Berlin Wall teaches us that change is possible, that barriers can be overcome, and that the human spirit is capable of extraordinary resilience in the face of adversity.

So let us not forget the lessons of history, but let us also look forward with hope and optimism to the future. Let us continue to strive for a world where walls are replaced with bridges, where divisions are healed, and where the ideals of freedom, democracy, and human dignity are upheld for all. And let us never lose sight of the fact that the power to shape the world lies not in the hands of governments or leaders, but in the hearts and minds of ordinary people like you and me.

Further Reading

1. "The Fall of the Berlin Wall: The Revolutionary Legacy of 1989" by Jeffrey A. Engel
2. "Iron Curtain: The Crushing of Eastern Europe, 1944-1956" by Anne Applebaum
3. "The Collapse: The Accidental Opening of the Berlin Wall" by Mary Elise Sarotte
4. "The File: A Personal History" by Timothy Garton Ash
5. "The Berlin Wall: A World Divided, 1961-1989" by Frederick Taylor
6. "The End of the Cold War: 1985-1991" by Robert Service
7. "Revolution 1989: The Fall of the Soviet Empire" by Victor Sebestyen
8. "Berlin 1961: Kennedy, Khrushchev, and the Most Dangerous Place on Earth" by Frederick Kempe
9. "The Wall: The Making of the Berlin Wall, 1961-1962" by Peter Wyden
10. "Checkpoint Charlie: The Cold War, the Berlin Wall, and the Most Dangerous Place on Earth" by Iain MacGregor

These books offer a comprehensive exploration of the fall of the Berlin Wall, the reunification of

Germany, and the broader historical context of the Cold War era. Whether you're a casual reader or a serious scholar, there's something here for everyone interested in delving deeper into this pivotal moment in modern history.